One Christmas Carol

Adapted for performance by

Douglas H. Baker

Based on the book A Christmas Carol by

Charles Dickens

STEELE SPRING STAGE RIGHTS

www.stagerights.com

For all stage performance inquiries, please contact:

STEELE SPRING
STAGE RIGHTS

Steele Spring Stage Rights
3845 Cazador Street
Los Angeles, CA 90065
(323) 739-0413
www.stagerights.com

CHARACTERS

The following is a description of the characters in the story in order of appearance. Each must be defined not only in attitude, intensity and purpose, but physically. The nature of this production requires quick transition from one character to the next.

It is important to note that some of the characters described below do not have dialogue in the play but are visually seen for brief moments. For this reason they are physically described here.

The Narration is used to allow characters to easily transition from one character to another. When the Narrator is himself only, he is the neutral character of the actor stepping out of the play for brief comments on the action of the story. In the script narration delivered in the physicality of a character is noted as such; example: Narr. as Bob.

NARRATOR is the neutral personality of the actor chosen for the play.

SCROOGE is a bit stiff, as if limited movement will waste less energy. He is tight both physically and money minded, self-confined in his own world, unable to adjust, not wanting to adjust, stubborn, determined to be stubborn, self-pitying only in an angry self-absorbed way, cautious and ready to pounce. He is afraid to feel and afraid of pain through a tender heart.

BOB CRATCHIT is a tall thin man, fragile in self-confidence, strong in spirituality, bounding with youthful spirit. He is sincere and loving, walks lightly and is timid. His power lies in his honest convictions and simple pleasures.

FRED is perpetually positive. He has a healthy happiness bursting with energy. He is romantic and handsome with pure mother's innocence. He is idealistic and hopeful for a better world. He is never a victim.

PORTLY GENT is never seen without his business companion. Whenever we see Portly Gent, he includes his partner in the conversation through eye contact and gesture. He is big-boned and blustery. He has a festive business demeanor, easily flustered, friendly but ineffective without the support of his partner.

BOY CAROLER is approximately 10 years old. He is diminutive, innocent, has a sweet sincerity and is a painter of beautiful imagery.

One Christmas Carol

CHARACTERS (CONT'D)

MARLEY is old, bound up, pulling himself along (opposite of dragging). He is worn out but driven, impatient, lonely, wanting and needing for himself. He has an urgent frustration, but reluctantly resigned to a constant heavy burden. It is important to play him with a desire for a better existence and not as a creature "beyond all hope."

CHRISTMAS PAST is described in the book as not old and not young. Christmas Past is neither male nor female. It is memories full either in joyful or painful experiences. This character never opens its eyes but uses grand gestures to physically embrace the positive memories with round open arms or push the negative memories physically away.

BOY SCROOGE is a comparable character to Boy Caroler. He is 12 years old, lonely, empty, longing, breathless and wanting.

FRAN is a little girl about 8 years old. She is playful and giving. Overly excited, exuberant and unable to stand still. Her bright-eyed energy is infectious. She is in a hurry, and will not be denied.

FEZZIWIG is a big, round, bouncy, lovably boisterous man. He is joyous of life at every moment, nurturing and huggable, willing to laugh at himself.

FEZZIWIG GUESTS are only small moments in the Fezziwig scene. They are moments of dancing, or cheering in differing qualities giving the scene the feeling of a party. Each moment of a character needs to have a simple but concrete tempo and intensity and physicality to depict varied characters in the warehouse.

BELLE is petite and lovely. She is lovingly sure, gentle, forgiving and humble yet never angry, but sad in her loss. She is resigned but firm in her resolve to end her relationship with Scrooge.

CHRISTMAS PRESENT is plenty and bursting with positive happy energy. This 'hope of new beginnings' has a huge, rich heart. He is bigger than life, proud and strong with little patience for Scrooge's pessimistic attitudes.

LOUD CHILDREN is one boisterous boy, a representative of a small group of child carolers singing a carol very loud and in haste. This single child sings with excitement, bouncing and bold, competing with his fellow carolers. They are completely in their own world.

One Christmas Carol

CHARACTERS (CONT'D)

MRS. CRATCHIT is fully a woman with a worn life experience. She is layered with responsibility and bravely embraces it. Physically quick, she is excitable, proud, loving and well kempt in her poverty. She has a slight biting protectiveness.

MARTHA is young in maturity— about 18 years old. She is sweet but still a girl, fun-loving and giggly. She is never physically still in her dialogue exchanges though she has a moderate level of young adulthood.

THE CHILDREN are a boy and a girl too young to be different in quality of character. They rush in, circling their mother and looking up at her, excited beyond control. They are seen again "placing chairs for everyone" and do this at breakneck speed with the clumsiness of reaction before planning.

BELINDA is the Cratchits' second daughter. She is old enough for responsibility but young enough to give in to the temptation of a sneaky taste of the applesauce.

PETER is a boy of about 14 trying to prove his capable hands. He fiercely mashes the potatoes as if racing to a finish line.

TINY TIM is a young, 6 year old boy. A symbol of love and innocence in a small, vulnerable, Godly package— smallest of them all with a big heart of pure love.

OLD MAN is experienced, wise and rich with swelling love for his family. He is tired but excepting, touching and embracing. He knows the importance beyond the veil of this life.

STURDY MAN is a tough hard worker, sure and hearty with a bit of a soft sentimental side.

MALE GUEST is a playboy, young and sneaky in a playful way.

PRETTY SISTER is giggly, coy and naive. She is shy and cute, and though she knows it and uses it, it is charming. She cannot stop giggling.

FEMALE GUEST is a sweet friend of Fred's wife. She is curious and competitive in game playing.

OLD MALE GUEST is a pipe smoking, logical and comfortable fellow.

GHOST OF CHRISTMAS FUTURE is never physically taken on by the actor but is a strong presence intently viewed by Scrooge. The image is of a heavily cloaked dark figure "concealing its head, face and form."

One Christmas Carol

CHARACTERS (CONT'D)

FAT MAN is an oily, large, greasy unmoved and uncaring man. He laughs at his own jokes and is callous and lumbering. He talks to a small group of other unseen businessmen.

OLD JOE is a squatty old codger, a brittle beggars vendee who thinks of himself as quite a player. Homely and somewhat toothless, he brazenly cowers in the darkness.

BEGGAR WOMAN is a cleaning lady and beggar woman full in age. A layered collector and protector of the clothes and wares she covets. She has a false unrepentant guilt.

YOUNG HUSBAND is romantic and genuinely loving, warm and protective. He has a sensual embracing oneness with his young wife. He is sincere about all his emotions.

STREET BOY is a young lad of about 10 years old. He is quick and eager.

SETTING

Christmas, Early 1800s

ACT I

Christmas, Early 1800s

The scenery consists of three unmatched chairs. The location of the story changes through the manipulation of these three chairs which constitute the entire set. CHAIR (1) is of a universal general nature, neither poor nor elegant. CHAIR (2) is SCROOGE's chair, somewhat nicer, yet clearly not costly. CHAIR (3) is BOB CRATCHIT's, worn but functional. The story begins in the counting house of SCROOGE and MARLEY.

STAVE I

Sound, 12 clock chimes begin.

1,2,3: lights begin to fade. 4,5,6,7: lights fade out.

8,9,10: lights fade up. Scrooge's office, chairs preset.

[DIAGRAM A]

SCROOGE is seated at his desk, chair (2) facing away from the audience, working diligently. 11, 12.

SCROOGE: Ah Humbug! Cratchit! *(Scrooge turns to Bob [Bob's chair (3)])* Stay to your work! You drift with the season! This miserable season of the year! Foolishness! Attend to your duties! It costs me money to watch you! It's dismal enough this time of year!

SCROOGE turns back to his work. He stops again shortly, turns quickly, stands and crosses toward BOB.

Stay to your work! There's money due from many and I want it marked today! Scrooge and Marley's is not a charitable institution, it is a business. It is my business! Now be quick about it.

SCROOGE returns to his chair (2).

NARR. AS SCROOGE: Scrooge went back to his desk and took only a moment to drown himself once again in his work.

NARRATOR stands and moves down stage to talk to audience.

NARRATOR: Bob Cratchit settled and, though preoccupied by the pending holiday celebration, focused hard on his duties, fearing Scrooge's often angry temper. Now let me make one thing clear. Marley was dead. People knew the business as Scrooge and Marley's. Scrooge answered to both names. It was all the same to him. But Marley was dead. There is no doubt... dead as a doornail. I don't mean to say that I know of my own knowledge, what there is dead about a doornail. I might have been inclined to say, "dead as a coffin nail," as the deadest piece of iron mongery. But,the phrase is done and I shall not disturb it. You will therefore permit me? To repeat emphatically, that Marley was dead... as a doornail.

Scrooge knew he was dead, yes, of course he did. He and Scrooge were partners. Scrooge was Marley's sole executor, his sole mourner, his sole... friend. And even Scrooge was not so dreadfully cut up on the day of the funeral... which only brings the point home... that Marley was dead... as a doornail. This point must be distinctly understood or nothing good will come of this story. Scrooge was tight fisted, as was Marley, and even more so after Marley's death.

SCROOGE crosses back to his chair (2).

NARR. AS SCROOGE: He was a squeezing, wrenching, grasping, covetous, solitary, sharp, shrewd, old, cold, bitter man.

SCROOGE scowls at the NARRATOR on the side of his chair.

SCROOGE: Ah Humbug!

The NARRATOR stands to the side of the chair, a little frightened of SCROOGE.

NARRATOR: No warmth could warm him, no winter weather chill him. And Christmas, well Christmas didn't thaw him one degree! Nobody ever stopped in the streets to talk or give him gladsome looks. No! His way was to warn all human sympathy away. The door to Scrooge's room in the counting house was kept open, that he might keep a strict eye on his clerk.

His clerk worked hard... possibly in effort to stay warm... for he had a small fire... smaller even than the small fire in Scrooge's room. But Scrooge kept the coal box in his room...

Cross and sit as BOB in chair (3).

NARR. AS BOB: ...and the clerk had not the courage or dared risk asking for more coal... so he warmed his hands a moment at the candle. *(Cross to stage right, open outside door and enter)* In that instant the outside door flew open.

Brief wind sound, door shut.

It was Scrooge's Nephew, Fred.

FRED enters and crosses to center.

FRED: A Merry Christmas Uncle! God save you!

SCROOGE steps out and stares at Fred.

SCROOGE: Bah! Humbug!

FRED: Christmas a Humbug! Surely you don't mean it, uncle! Oh, it is cold with frost and fog, true... but nothing in this could spoil the season.

FRED moves chair (1) from the door to the window and stands on it to open the window curtains.

Curtain slide.

That crisp cold air has never felt warmer. Come, look at it uncle, all aglow with hope and joy and glad tidings.

FRED steps off chair (1), crosses to Scrooge.

NARRATOR: But Scrooge having no better answer... on the spur of the moment... said...

SCROOGE turns toward FRED.

SCROOGE: Bah! Humbug!

FRED: Don't be cross, Uncle!

SCROOGE: What else can I be... when I live in a world of fools such as this? Out upon Merry Christmas!

SCROOGE (CONT'D): What's Christmas time to you but a time for paying bills without money, a time for finding yourself another year older but not an hour richer. If I could work my will, every idiot who goes about with Merry Christmas on his lips should be boiled in his own pudding.

Nephew... you keep Christmas in your way and I shall keep it in mine.

FRED: Keep it! Uncle, you don't keep it! *(Fred crosses down left, to the side of Bob [3])* You don't keep it at all. Christmas is a good time, a kind, forgiving charitable time, the only time I know of in the long calendar year when men and women open their shut-up hearts... freely... and think of others as fellow passengers to the grave. There are many things from which I have not profited... Christmas among the rest. And therefore, uncle... I believe, though it has not put a penny in my pocket, that it has done me good... and will do me good— and I say, God Bless it!

BOB sits quickly on chair (3) and applauds.

NARR. AS BOB: The clerk in the adjoining room applauded involuntarily and Scrooge turned in anger and said.

SCROOGE stands, he points at BOB in anger.

SCROOGE: Let me hear one more word out of you and you will celebrate by losing your position. So... my meddling nephew is quite a speaker. Your speech has inspired one... one who has little chance of bettering his situation. But... you waste my time. Good day!

SCROOGE turns and begins to cross to his desk. FRED stops and turns front.

FRED: Well sir... I... I speak from my heart. I do not mean to offend you. I simply fear you may be lonely this time of year. What, with Marley gone! *(Fred turns to Scrooge)* Come... dine with us tomorrow.

NARRATOR: But Scrooge frowned harshly and said...

SCROOGE turns quickly.

SCROOGE: I will first see you in...

NARRATOR: ...but, he used the entire expression ... and then he said...

SCROOGE: Good afternoon!

FRED: I am sorry uncle, with all my heart, to find you so resolute. We have never had a quarrel. I want nothing from you... I ask nothing of you... why can we not be friends? *(Fred waits for an answer)* Well... Well... I have made this trial in homage to Christmas, and I shall keep my Christmas humor to the last. So, Merry Christmas, Uncle... and a Happy New Year!

SCROOGE watches Fred as he moves toward Bob (3).

SCROOGE: Humbug! Humbug!... Love... love has made him giddy! A new wife— as if that were the only thing in the world.

FRED shakes BOB's hand.

NARR. AS FRED: Fred stopped to wish Bob Cratchit the best of the season... who, as cold as he was, was warmer than Scrooge.

SCROOGE crosses back to center while watching his foolish clerk.

SCROOGE: There's another fellow: my clerk, with fifteen schillings a week, and a wife... and family... talking about a Merry Christmas. Humbug!

NARR. AS SCROOGE: Again the outside door flew open...

Wind in.

FRED passes through the door.

NARR. AS FRED: ...As Fred passed through...

PORTLY GENTLEMEN enters it is as if he (they) had to squeeze past Fred.

NARR. AS PORTLY GENTLEMEN: ...As two portly gentlemen entered.

Wind out, door shut.

They stood... With their hats off... patiently waiting. They bowed. One of them spoke up, cheerfully.

PORTLY GENTLMEN: Have we the pleasure of addressing Mr. Scrooge or Mr. Marley?

SCROOGE: Marley's dead... seven years, *(Under his breath)* Idiots!

SCROOGE replaces chair (1) by the door to the counting house. HE is annoyed as the two Gentlemen are in his way. PORTLY GENTLEMEN speak after the chair is replaced.

PORTLY GENTLMEN: Well, we're very sorry Mr. Scrooge. In this festive season of the year, Mr. Scrooge, it is more-than-usually desirable that we should make some slight provisions for the poor and destitute, who suffer greatly at the present time. *(Pause for an answer, none is given)* ...Many, sir, are in want of common comforts. A few of us are endeavoring to raise a fund... to buy the poor some meat and drink and means of warmth. We wish to know, sir, what we can put you down for.

SCROOGE crosses up to his desk.

SCROOGE: Are there no prisons? And the union workhouses, are they still in operation?

PORTLY GENTLEMEN backs away slightly flustered.

PORTLY GENTLMEN: Oh, yes, sir, there are plenty of prisons and workhouses, though we wish we could say there were none. Both are very busy.

SCROOGE continues to his desk.

SCROOGE: Good! I'm glad to hear it! I Shall give you nothing! You ask what I wish, gentlemen— that is my answer. I don't make merry at Christmas. I can't afford to make others merry. I help support those establishments. They cost enough, let the poor go there.

PORTLY GENTLEMEN crosses down stage, flustered.

PORTLY GENTLMEN: Many cannot go there, sir! And many would rather die!

SCROOGE turns quickly toward PORTLY GENTLEMEN.

SCROOGE: Well then, let them do it— and decrease the surplus population! Good afternoon, gentlemen!

PORTLY GENTLMEN *(as if speaking to his partner beside him)*: Well!

NARR. AS PORTLY GENTLEMEN: Well, seeing clearly it was useless to pursue the point, the gentlemen withdrew...

Brief wind, door shut.

SCROOGE starts to his desk but is drawn to the front window.

NARRATOR: ...And Scrooge resumed his labors. The cold outside and inside was intense...

BOB crosses to chair (3).

NARR. AS BOB: ...and Bob felt it burning on his fingertips. *(Bob's attention is drawn to the front door. He crosses to the door)* But he was warmed for a short time by a small boy singing at Scrooge's keyhole.

BOY CAROLER is standing on the outside of the door, he sings:

BOY CAROLER:

GOD REST YE MERRY GENTLEMEN
LET NOTHING YOU DISMAY
REMEMBER CHRIST OUR SAVIOR
WAS BORN ON CHRISTMAS DAY
TO SAVE US ALL FROM SATAN'S POWER
WHEN WE HAD GONE ASTRAY
OH, TIDINGS OF COMFORT AND JOY
COMFORT AND JOY
OH, TIDINGS OF COMFORT AND...

Wind in.

SCROOGE quickly opens the counting house door and screams.

SCROOGE: Get out of here you little brat!

Wind out, door shut. SCROOGE watches the Boy run away.

NARR. AS SCROOGE: Scrooge had frightened the boy away and when he returned to his work found his clerk preparing to leave for his Christmas holiday. Well... well, so I see you have wasted no time.

BOB: It is past our closing hour, sir. *(Bob puts away his chair (3) by the door, left of chair (1))* I'm sorry sir.

SCROOGE: Yes, I'm sure you are. You'll want all day tomorrow, I suppose?

BOB: If convenient, sir?

SCROOGE: Well, it's not convenient and it's not fair. If I should stop half a crown for it, you'd think yourself ill used, yet you don't think me ill used when I pay a day's wages for no work. Still, I suppose you must have the whole day. Be here all the earlier the next morning.

NARR. AS BOB: The clerk promised he would. *(Bob crosses to chair (3))* Then he wrapped himself in a long white scarf... for he boasted no coat... *(Bob leaves the counting house)* ...nor did he need one, not today, for he was filled with the Christmas spirit. *(Bob goes out into the street)* He went down a slide on corn hill with other boys— twenty times on account of it being Christmas eve and then he skipped through the streets warmed by the promise of the Christmas spirit and a loving family waiting sweetly at home.

NARR. AS SCROOGE: Scrooge took his melancholy dinner... alone and beguiled the rest of the evening with his bankers books and went home to bed. He lived in chambers which had once belonged to his deceased partner. *(Crosses into his own yard and to his front door stage left)* They were a gloomy set of rooms in a pile of buildings where they had little business to be. The yard was dark and Scrooge, who knew its every footfall moved unassuredly to his door.

SCROOGE'S ROOM

NARRATOR: Now, it is a fact that there was nothing unusual about the knocker on the door, except that it was large. In fact, Scrooge had seen it night and morning during his whole residence in the place...

NARR. AS SCROOGE: ...But this time, as he placed his key into the lock of the door... *(Key in lock, turning)* ...he saw Marley's face. It was not angry or ferocious but clearly the ghostly look of Marley. What is this? He that is seven years dead! He looked again but it was a knocker again. To say he was merely startled would be untrue. He placed his hand back upon the key... *(Key in lock, turning)* ...turned the lock, opened the door... peeked behind it... and sturdily walked in and lighted a candle.

SCROOGE quickly lights a candle, turns back to the door and exams it in the candle light.

SCROOGE: Pooh! Pooh! It's humbug! Humbug, I tell you!

NARRATOR: Now, the truth is darkness is cheap, so Scrooge liked it!

NARR. AS SCROOGE: But, he shut the door for the recollection of the face gave him desire to do so. He locked himself in... *(Slide lock)* ...double locked himself in. *(Slide lock, Scrooge walks around his rooms)* His sitting room... dining room, all as they should be. No-one under the table, no one behind the sofa, he put on his dressing gown and his night cap...

SCROOGE moves chair (2) to the fireplace in SCROOGE's room and sits (chairs (1) & (3) represent the fireplace).

[DIAGRAM B]

NARR. AS SCROOGE (CONT'D): ...attended to a small fire and sat down to eat his evening gruel.

SCROOGE: Ha! It was nothing!

NARR. AS SCROOGE: And so began an uneventful evening.

Old bell.

Soon! Very soon, he heard a bell,

Old bell.

...an old bell...

Old bell.

...a disused bell. A bell of some consequence now forgot which presently began to ring...

Many bells.

...and before long all the bells in the house began to ring, and as quickly as they started they ceased.

Bells out, chains in.

He heard a clanking noise deep down below, as if a person were dragging a chain toward him.

SCROOGE: It's humbug! I won't believe it! Humbug!

SCROOGE sees MARLEY pass through the door down left.

NARR. AS SCROOGE: But before he finished his last humbug, a ghost passed through the door and a screech of sound both Scrooge and fear itself exclaimed.

Chains out.

SCROOGE: Aaagh! I know him! It's Marley's ghost!

Chains in. MARLEY drags his chain.

NARR. AS MARLEY: The chain the ghost drew was clasp about his middle and wound around him like a tail. It was made of cash boxes, keys and padlocks, of ledgers, deeds and heavy, heavy purses, all transparent.

Chains out. SCROOGE steps out of MARLEY.

NARR. AS SCROOGE: He was transparent! Scrooge even observed the two buttons on his coat... behind him. Scrooge felt the chilling influence of his death cold eyes and he coward at the apparition.

Chains in. MARLEY steps out of SCROOGE.

NARR. AS MARLEY: The ghost moved forward in slow motion and addressed the frightened Scrooge.

MARLEY: In life I was your partner, Jacob Marley. Why? Why do you look so dull man? You don't believe in me. Why do you doubt your senses?

Chains out.

NARR. AS SCROOGE: Scrooge protested strongly... then cautiously.

SCROOGE: I don't know! Because a slight disorder of the stomach makes them cheat. You may be a bit of undigested beef, or a crumb of cheese or a fragment of underdone potato. There's more gravy than grave about you.

SCROOGE has moved to chair (2) and is seated by the fireplace.

NARR. AS SCROOGE: Scrooge was not in the habit of cracking jokes, nor was he waggish. The truth was, he tried to be smart to keep down his terror.

SCROOGE: It's humbug! Humbug, I tell you!

Chains in.

NARR. AS MARLEY: And with this the spirit rose up and shook his chain, aaagh...

MARLEY stands and shakes his chain. Chains out.

NARR. AS SCROOGE: ...and Scrooge, wishing to save himself, fell from his chair in a swoon.

SCROOGE falls to the floor in front of him.

SCROOGE: Mercy spirit, mercy! I do believe in you— I must— but why do you walk the earth and why have you come to me?

NARRATOR: The spirit, having Scrooge's full attention made firm his purpose.

Chains in. MARLEY stands.

MARLEY: It is required of every man that the spirit within him shall walk among his fellow men, and if that spirit goes not forth in life it is condemned to do so after death and witness what it cannot share but might have shared and turned to happiness. I wear the chain I forged in life. I made it link by link, yard by yard. I would you know the length of your own chain, it was full and heavy as this seven Christmas eves ago.

Chains out.

NARR. AS SCROOGE: Scrooge looked around himself, expecting to see but seeing nothing.

SCROOGE: Jacob! Speak comfort to me Jacob! Speak comfort!

Chains in.

MARLEY: I cannot stay! I cannot linger anywhere! I cannot rest! My spirit never walked beyond the four walls of our counting house! My spirit never roved beyond our money changing hands.

Chains out.

SCROOGE: Well Jacob, you might have gone over a great quantity of ground over the last seven years... you always were a good man of business.

Chains in.

MARLEY: Business... Business... Mankind was my business. Charity, mercy, forbearance were all my business. In this festive season of the year I suffer most, but hear me, my time is nearly gone. How I appear in shape before you I may not tell. I have sat invisible beside you many and many a day.

Chains out.

NARR. AS SCROOGE: This was not an agreeable idea to Scrooge, who wiped the perspiration from his brow.

Chains in.

MARLEY: I am here tonight to warn you... That you have yet a chance of escaping my fate. Ebenezer... you will be haunted by three spirits.

Chains in.

NARR. AS SCROOGE: Scrooge's countenance fell as low as before.

SCROOGE: Is that the chance... The chance you speak of... I think I'd rather not!

Chains in.

MARLEY: Aaagh! Without their visits you cannot hope to shun the path I tread.

MARLEY begins to move the chairs from the fireplace to assemble the bed, chair (2).

[DIAGRAM C]

Expect the first tomorrow when the bell tolls one.

Chains out.

SCROOGE: Couldn't I take them all at once, Jacob, and get it over with?

Chains in.

MARLEY: No! *(Marley moves chair (3) to become part of the bed)* Expect the second on the next night at the same hour and the third... *(Marley moves chair (1) to become part of the bed)* ...upon the next when the last stroke of twelve shall vibrate... and remember what has passed between us.

Chains out. MARLEY steps back and disappears into darkness.

NARR. AS MARLEY: And with this the spirit stepped back into the incoherent wailing's of regret that joined in the mournful dirge that floated elsewhere out upon the bleak dark night.

SCROOGE rushes forward. We are now in his bedroom.

SCROOGE: Humbug! Humbug! Hum...

NARR. AS SCROOGE: Perhaps it was the fatigue of the day... or the lateness of the hour... or the dull conversation of the ghost, for Scrooge went straight to bed... *(Scrooge crosses to bed)* ...without undressing... was Marley a dream... or was he not!

NARR. AS SCROOGE (CONT'D): Scrooge lay in this state of wonder for three quarters of an hour and then remembered on a sudden the ghost warning of a visitation when the bell tolled one. He resolved to remain awake until the hour.

DIRECT SEGUE INTO STAVE II

STAVE II

SCROOGE'S BEDROOM

NARR. AS SCROOGE: The quarter was so long...

Bell.

...and then the bell, the hour itself and nothing more. No longer than an instant followed and a light flashed up in the room.

Twinkle chime.

And standing before him was a strange figure... like a child... yet, not so like a child... as like an old man... yet, not old.

SCROOGE: Are you the spirit, Sir, whose coming was foretold to me? Who and what are you?

PAST stands and pulls Scrooge from the bed.

PAST: I am the ghost of Christmas Past. Your past! I am here for your welfare, your reclamation. Take heed, rise and walk with me!

Isolated scene down right:

Open country road, no chair change.

NARR. AS SCROOGE: Scrooge took the ghost's hand— fearfully. He knew it was in vain to resist, and in a blink of the eyes...

Twinkle chime.

...found they stood on an open country road. It was a clear, cold day and there was snow on the ground.

SCROOGE: Good heavens! I was bred in this place. I was a boy here!

NARR. AS SCROOGE: Scrooge was conscious of a thousand odors floating in the air, each one connected to a thousand thoughts... and hopes and joys... and... well, cares... yes, cares, cares, long forgotten! He saw many boys he knew and he waved to them.

SCROOGE: I remember this place! I could walk it blindfolded!

PAST: These are but the shadows of the things that have been. They have no consciousness of us.

NARR AS PAST: And with this the two turned to see.

Twinkle chime.

Isolated scene, stage left:

SCROOGE'S BOYHOOD SCHOOL

No chair change.

PAST: The school is not quite deserted. A solitary child... neglected by friends and family is left there still. A small boy is sitting by a feeble fire. Do you see yourself as you once were?

BOY SCROOGE seated on the floor sings "God Rest Ye Merry Gentlemen" while attending the fire.

BOY SCROOGE:
GOD REST YE MERRY GENTLEMEN
LET NOTHING YOU DISMAY
REMEMBER CHRIST OUR SAVIOR
WAS BORN ON CHRISTMAS DAY

BOY SCROOGE stops, he thinks he hears his friends but he is wrong. He continues singing sadly.

TO SAVE US ALL FROM SATAN'S POWER
WHEN WE HAD GONE ASTRAY
OH, TIDINGS OF COMFORT AND JOY
COMFORT AND JOY
OH, TIDINGS OF COMFORT AND...

SCROOGE stands watching the boy.

NARR AS SCROOGE: Scrooge listened a long time after the boy had finished and then he said,

SCROOGE: Tonight, a boy was singing outside my shop. I wish I... had given him something.

PAST: Yes, let us see another Christmas.

Twinkle chime. PAST crosses to an imaginary door, stage right, of the school.

NARR AS PAST: The door to the school opened...

NARR. AS FRAN: ...and in rushed a little girl, younger than the boy.

FRAN rushes in, center stage, jumping and dancing excitedly around Boy Scrooge.

FRAN: Brother! Dear, dear brother! I have come to bring you home, home, home, for good and all. Home forever and ever! *(Fran stops and stares lovingly at her brother)* Father is so much kinder that home is like heaven and you're to be a man and never come back here and we're to be together the whole Christmas long and have the merriest time in all the world! Oh, come Ebenezer, come... come... come!

SCROOGE: Oh... generous ghost! To see my dear, sweet little sister Fran, always a delicate creature whom a breath might have withered. She died a woman, had but one child, my nephew... Fred— *(Disgustedly)* —ha!

Twinkle chime.

CHRISTMAS PAST walks through the city to behind the warehouse (represented by the bed).

NARR. AS PAST: Soon, the two walked on through the shadowy thoroughfares of a city and stopped at a certain warehouse door. It was evening and the streets were lighted up.

CHRISTMAS PAST separates chair (1) creating a door to FEZZIWIG's warehouse.

[DIAGRAM D]

PAST: Do you know this?

SCROOGE: Know this! I apprenticed here!

Twinkle chime. SCROOGE crosses into FEZZIWIG's warehouse between the chairs (door).

FEZZIWIG'S WAREHOUSE

NARR. AS SCROOGE: As they went in, Scrooge stared up at the old Welsh gentlemen who was sitting behind the high desk.

SCROOGE: Why it's old Fezziwig! Imagine, Fezziwig alive again. Bless his heart!

FEZZIWIG, downstage, behind his desk.

NARR. AS FEZZIWIG: Old Fezziwig looked up at the clock and rubbed his hands together and called out in a comfortable, oily, rich, fat, jovial voice.

FEZZIWIG: Yo Ho there, Ebenezer, no more work tonight! It's Christmas eve! Hilli-ho, cheery up there Ebenezer, cheery up! Clear away, clear away!

FEZZIWIG clears chair (2) to down right, later used for Belle scene.

[DIAGRAM E]

NARR. AS SCROOGE: And it was done in a minute. Every moveable was packed away and the warehouse was snug and warm. *(Scrooge, upright, watches as the imaginary characters enter)* In came the fiddler and Mrs. Fezziwig, beaming and lovable. In came the house keeper with her cousin, the baker. In came the cook with her brother's particular friend... the milkman... Huh...

Multiple characters go in and out of the dance. There is a sense of a big party ending this next speech with SCROOGE in the same place up right, excited and out of breath.

And they danced boldly... gracefully... awkwardly. And Fezziwig and Mrs. Fezziwig had gone all through the dance and everyone cried, "most wonderful, most excellent," bow and curtsey, corkscrew, thread the needle and back again. And Fezziwig— Fezziwig, cut so deftly that he appeared to wink with his legs and come upon his feet again without a stagger. And during the whole scene, Scrooge acted like a man out of his wits, his heart and soul were in the scene and with his former self.

Twinkle chime. PAST steps right of SCROOGE, giggling.

PAST: Ha, Ha! A small matter, said the ghost... to these silly people, so full of gratitude. Why? Why does he deserve your change of heart? He wasted pounds of your mortal money. Too much to waste on a mere party!

SCROOGE steps left of PAST and is drawn downstage by his realizations.

SCROOGE: No! Not too much! More than money! He had the power to render us happy! Power lies in looks. In deeds! In things so slight and insignificant... that it is impossible to add and count them up. The happiness he gave is quite as much as if it cost a fortune!... *(Scrooge crosses back up right to address Past)* Spirit! I should like to have a word with my clerk just now!

PAST steps away.

PAST: Of course, but my time grows short and there is more to see. Come quickly.

Cymbal and bow.

NARR. AS SCROOGE *(Scrooge in his late 20s)*: Scrooge saw himself older now, a man in the prime of life, but this time there was a greedy motion in his eyes... and he was not alone, but in the company of a fair young girl.

SCROOGE turns to his left addressing CHRISTMAS PAST, desperate to escape.

SCROOGE: Oh spirit, do not lead me to this place!

PAST: The choices you made in life were yours to make, now to unfold. Do you wish they had been different?

SCROOGE: I was afraid... of losing... of losing... my position, my work, my business! It was mine to keep, mine to secure. A man cannot depend on another's charity! He must take care of himself!

PAST: True enough! But, what of Belle?

SCROOGE: Love is not enough!... Love is not! Love is... Belle.

Twinkle chime. BELLE crosses to the chair and sits.

NARR. AS BELLE: Belle, in whose eyes there were tears.

BELLE: It matters little, Oh Ebenezer, very little to you. Another idol has displaced me, and if it can comfort you in times to come, I have no just cause to grieve. You fear the world too much, Ebenezer. I have seen your nobler aspirations fall. I am a witness of neglect and false hope. You have a mistress and her name is gain and she has engrossed you. *(Belle stands and crosses behind chair (2))* As I love you, I release you. *(Belle begins to leave through the door of Fezziwig's warehouse.)* May you truly be happy in the life you have chosen. Farewell, Ebenezer, farewell...

Cymbal and bow.

SCROOGE: No more! Show me no more! Remove me from this place...

SCROOGE unwittingly replaces chair (2) in between chairs (1 & 3) to recreate bed, back in SCROOGE's bedroom.

[DIAGRAM C]

SCROOGE'S BEDROOM

SCROOGE: ...remove me, for I cannot bear this... I cannot bear it!

NARR. AS SCROOGE: Scrooge was conscious of being exhausted and barely found his bed...

Cymbal and bow.

...before he sank into a heavy, heartfelt sleep.

SEGUE INTO STAVE III

STAVE III

SCROOGE'S BEDROOM

One clock chime.

NARR. AS SCROOGE *(rough snore)*: Awaking from a prodigiously tough snore, Scrooge had no occasion to be told the bell was once again upon the stroke of one. He quickly established a sharp lookout around the room. I don't mind calling on you to believe, he was ready for a good, broad field of strange appearances and nothing between a baby and a rhinoceros would have surprised him very much. But, being prepared for anything... He was not now prepared for nothing. Five... ten... A quarter of an hour went by... still nothing. Yet, all this time, a ruddy dim light was streaming from beneath the door of the adjoining room. Scrooge, finally, shuffled to the door and opened it.

SCROOGE moves down right to open door, the imaginary next room is down center.

Twinkle chime.

The walls and ceiling were alive with greenery, from every part of which bright, gleaming berries glistened. There was holly and mistletoe and ivy, and a blazing fire which Scrooge's hearth had never seen. Heaped on the floor, forming a throne upon which the ghost...

Twinkle chime.

...was seated, were turkeys and suckling pigs, wreaths of sausages, mince pies and plum puddings, apples, pears and juicy oranges, all in a shape not unlike plenty's horn.

Twinkle chime. CHRISTMAS PRESENT steps center front. He is very big in stature and personality.

CHRISTMAS PRESENT: Come in! Come in, and know me better, man! You have never seen the likes of me before or of my brothers before me. There have been hundreds and hundreds of them.

SCROOGE: A tremendous family to provide for, spirit! You are the second spirit! I am in a receptive mood, spirit. Take me where you will, tonight, if you will. Let me profit by it, for I assure you, I am now ready to learn.

CHRISTMAS PRESENT: Ha! HA! HA! Then come man! Touch my robe!

Twinkle chime, slow quiet wind in.

Scrooge steps back quickly into city streets, no chair change.

NARR. AS SCROOGE: And with nothing more, they stood in the city streets. The weather was severe. The house fronts looked bleak, the sky was gloomy and yet there was an air of cheerfulness. For the people called out to one another and exchanged better natured snowballs, laughing heartily when they went right.

Wind out.

NARR. AS SCROOGE (CONT'D): And children, children sang a Christmas carol, much too loud, yet happily.

BOY CAROLER steps forward, singing and dancing loudly.

BOY CAROLER:
GOOD KING WENCESLAS LOOKED OUT
ON THE FEAST OF STEPHEN
WHEN THE SNOW LAY ROUND ABOUT
DEEP AND CRISP AND EVEN

SCROOGE stumbles back and then notices the grocer's shop down right.

NARR. AS SCROOGE: And the grocers! Oh! The grocers, nearly closed, with perhaps two shutters down... but through those gaps, such glimpses! All there was good to eat in its Christmas dress and everyone in their best humor.

Church bells ring. SCROOGE crosses down left.

And soon the steeple called all good people to church and chapel, and away they came, flocking through the streets, dressed in their best and with their gayest faces.

Church bells stop. SCROOGE looks upstage toward the imaginary church and then forward at the imaginary street.

And then the bells ceased! And then for a time... all was quiet... With no one about to see the picture of beauty that lay before them.

Church bells ring.

And then the bells!

Church bells stop.

And then the bells ceased! And the bakers' shops emptied of their freshly cooked feasts, and the dinners now in progress, and the street cold, yet, warm with joyful wonder.

SCROOGE at center stage, he circles upstage to Christmas Present, stage right of the chairs.

SCROOGE: It marvels me, said Scrooge! It marvels me, that so many with so little have no fear of tomorrow. Forgive me, spirit, forgive me, for I have looked at this before... but I have not seen!

CHRISTMAS PRESENT moves chair (1) to create the Cratchit home (DIAGRAM F).

NARR. AS CHRISTMAS PRESENT: Perhaps it was pleasure or sympathy for all poor men, for the spirit lead the way to the threshold of a door. He stopped to bless Bob Cratchit's house.

Twinkle chime. CHRISTMAS PRESENT at the Cratchit front door.

CHRISTMAS PRESENT: Come, let us go in.

SCROOGE: Oh no, spirit! I have no need to see this dwelling. What have I to learn here?

CHRISTMAS PRESENT: Why do you protest? Because you feel remorse. You think if you close your eyes, you cannot see... you cannot hear... you cannot feel. Open your eyes, man, and become more than you were a moment ago.

Twinkle chime.

CRATCHIT HOME

CHRISTMAS PRESENT sits on chair (1), facing upstage. MRS. CRATCHIT rises from chair (1).

NARR. AS MRS. CRATCHIT: Mrs. Cratchit rose up, dressed out poorly in a twice turned gown brave in ribbons. She was assisted by her second daughter, Belinda, while master Peter Cratchit plunged a fork in the sauce pan. Two younger Cratchit's came tearing in, screaming...

CRATCHIT CHILD circles his/her imaginary mother dancing and squealing.

CRATCHIT CHILDREN: ...mother, mother, outside the butcher shop we can smell the goose, we can smell the goose!

MRS. CRATCHIT, in the center between the two imaginary, children is laughing.

MRS. CRATCHIT: Oh my ! Oh my, my! Where is your father— and your brother, Tiny Tim. And Martha, Martha was not so late last Christmas by half an hour. *(Mrs. Cratchit by the front door)* Oh, praise the day, here's Martha now. Why, bless your heart. How late you are my dear, let me look at you and kiss you... you're freezing! Come, sit down by the fire and have yourself a warm. Lord bless ye.

MARTHA plops down on the small sofa, chairs (2) & (3).

MARTHA: Oh, we'd a deal of work to do last night and had to clear away this morning. But at last its done and we're all together. Mother, I may be late but I'm not as late as father. I think I saw him coming just behind me.

NARR. AS MARTHA: And with this, all the children cried, "Hide, Martha, hide."

MARTHA rushes behind the couch, BOB enters across the back as if entering the house through the back door.

NARR. AS BOB: Shortly, Bob came in. His clothes were threadbare but he was smiling, with Tiny Tim upon his shoulders. Alas, poor Tiny Tim, for he supported a little crutch with an iron frame.

BOB CRATCHIT: Happy days, my dears. Happy days... Why, where's Martha... not coming on Christmas day.

MARTHA jumps out center.

NARR. AS MARTHA: But Martha jumped out and all began to laugh and hug...

MARTHA: ...for such a secret cannot be kept on such a joyous day.

BOB addresses Mrs. Cratchit down right by chair (1).

BOB CRATCHIT: All of us! All of us together! It is truly a blessing that warms a father's heart. Mother, Tiny Tim was as good as gold... and better. He told me in church, he hoped the people saw him, that it might be pleasant for them to remember on Christmas day who it was that made blind men see and lame beggars walk.

NARR. AS BOB: And with that the small and meager home became a bustle of hurry.

PETER rushes left of center.

NARR. AS PETER CRATCHIT: Master Peter Cratchit mashed the potatoes...

BELINDA rushes right of center.

NARR. AS BELINDA: ...While Belinda sweetened the applesauce...

YOUNGER CRATCHITS place chairs (2) & (3).

[DIAGRAM G]

NARR. AS CRATCHIT CHILDREN: ...As the two younger Cratchit's placed chairs for everyone and then put spoons in their mouths lest they shriek with excitement.

BOB crosses to front of imaginary table, surrounded by the chairs.

NARRATOR: At last, the dishes were set and grace was said, and never was there such a goose. Oh, it was small but there was enough for everyone.

MRS. CRATCHIT backing out up left to retrieve plum pudding.

NARR. AS MRS. CRATCHIT: And Mrs. Cratchit, fearing the plum pudding success, left the room to retrieve it...

NARR. AS CRATCHIT CHILDREN: ...And all sat in breathless anticipation...

Twinkle chime. MRS. CRATCHIT returns to BOB's side.

NARR. AS MRS. CRATCHIT: ...but she returned smiling proudly...

BOB acknowledges his wife.

NARRATOR: ...and it was wonderful. In a toast to the day, each Cratchit careworn... to the youngest, raised their tumblers and custard cups, as golden goblets would have done.

BOB CRATCHIT: A Merry Christmas, my dears! God bless us!

NARRATOR: Which the whole family echoed but just as they raised their cups to drink, Tiny Tim in a small but spirited voice broke out in deafening clarity.

Finger cymbals. TINY TIM steps forward and sits on chair (1) facing away from the audience. TINY TIM extends his right arm boyishly into the air.

TINY TIM: God bless us, everyone!

A young laugh to an old laugh transitioning from TINY TIM to SCROOGE.

SCROOGE getting up from the chair crosses center, referring back to Tiny Tim.

SCROOGE: Tiny Tim, ha! ha! Tiny... Tim... Tell me spirit, will Tiny Tim live?

CHRISTMAS PRESENT turns and crosses down left to fireplace.

[DIAGRAM F]

CHRISTMAS PRESENT: I see an empty chair in a poor chimney corner and a crutch without an owner. If these shadows remain unchanged, the boy will die.

SCROOGE: No! No, kind spirit! Say it is not so!

CHRISTMAS PRESENT: If he be like to die, he'd better do it and decrease the surplus population.

NARR. AS SCROOGE: Scrooge hung his head to hear his own words and was overcome with penitence and grief. But the spirit of Christmas Present stood strong.

CHRISTMAS PRESENT circles Scrooge who is center stage; HE circles to chair (3).

[DIAGRAM G]

CHRISTMAS PRESENT: Will you decide which men shall live and which men shall die? It may be in the sight of god that you are more worthless and less fit to live than millions like this poor man's child.

Wind in. NARRATOR moves chair (3) to Miner's Camp: isolated area down left.

[DIAGRAM G-2]

NARR. AS SCROOGE: Scrooge grasped the ghost's robe and together they whisked off to a place where miners live...

NARR. AS OLD MAN: ...Passing through a wall of mud and stone, to a cheerful fire with an old man...

OLD MAN sits, acknowledging his wife to his left, his children to his right and his grandchildren in front of him. During the song he relates to each of them lovingly.

And an old woman... And their children... And their children's children, all gathered round, protecting the glowing flame from the howling by.

Wind fade away.

The old man, in a voice calm and sweet, sang a Christmas carol, old, from when he was a boy.

OLD MAN sings.

OLD MAN:
WHAT CHILD IS THIS
WHO LAID TO REST
ON MARY'S LAP IS SLEEPING
WHOM ANGELS GREET WITH ANTHEMS SWEET
WHILE SHEPHERDS WATCH ARE KEEPING
THIS, THIS IS CHRIST THE KING
WHOM SHEPHERDS GUARD AND ANGELS SING
HASTE, HASTE TO BRING HIM LAUDE
THE BABE, THE SON OF MARY

Twinkle chime followed by wind growing. NARRATOR moves chair (2) to light house: isolated area.

[DIAGRAM G-3]

NARRATOR: But the spirit did not tarry and the two traveled to the sea, across deafening thunder of water to a lighthouse sitting alone on a dismal reef of sunken rock.

Light wind.

NARR. AS STURDY MAN: Here, even here! The two men who watched the light, joined hands across a rough table and wished each other...

STURDY MAN: ...A Merry Christmas!

Wind out.

NARR. AS STURDY MAN: The elder, his face damaged and scared by hard weather, struck up a sturdy tune.

STURDY MAN leans back in his chair, he sings.

STURDY MAN:
GOOD CHRISTIAN MEN REJOICE
WITH HEART AND SOUL AND VOICE
GIVE YE HEED TO WHAT WE SAY
JESUS CHRIST IS BORN TODAY
CHRIST IS BORN TODAY
CHRIST IS BORN TODAY

Light wind in.

NARRATOR moves chair (2) to create a ship, up right and leans over the chair.

[DIAGRAM G-4)

NARR. AS SCROOGE: But again the two sped on... on to a ship, and looking below could hear every man hum a Christmas tune. And then in a wink—

Wind out.

NARR. AS SCROOGE (CONT'D): –Scrooge found himself elsewhere, yet again. He heard a hearty laugh he knew... It was his nephew's...

Twinkle chime.

FRED'S HOUSE

They had come to his nephew's.

FRED crosses center, laughing.

FRED: Ha! Ha! Ha! Ha! He said, Christmas is a humbug, as I live, and he believed it too! My uncle is a comical old fellow, and not so pleasant as he might seem. His wealth is of no use to him, he doesn't do any good with it. He doesn't make himself comfortable. But I am sorry for him. He takes it into his head to dislike us. What's the consequence? He doesn't lose much of a dinner. *(Fred begs forgiveness from his wife seated facing him in chair left)* Ha! Ha! I'm sorry my dear. He loses a very good dinner! Ha! Ha! *(Fred crosses back center)* Oh! I mean to give him the same chance every year, whether he likes it or not. If it only puts him in the vain to leave his poor clerk fifty pounds, well, that's something.

FRED crosses to his wife in chair left. He moves chair (1) to right side of chair (2), He dances with his wife to center. SCROOGE emerges up center and watches the party

[DIAGRAM H]

NARR. AS FRED: Fred moved sweetly to his young and beautiful wife and, together with their friends, they later celebrated with singing and dancing and playing games.

NARR. AS SCROOGE: Scrooge began to feel as though he were part of the mood. He watched as they played blind mans bluff... and marveled at how one young fellow, whom all evening, held fast his attention to the pretty sister of Fred's wife...

MALE GUEST, blindfolded, moves to sit on chair (2). IMAGINARY PRETTY SISTER is on chair (1).

NARR. AS MALE GUEST: ...made each bob and turn, never losing sight of her, though blindfolded, until he found her and was rewarded with a giggle and a kiss upon the cheek. And then the fellow said...

MALE GUEST: Let's play another game, Fred. You pick it! You always pick something funny!

FRED steps center, FEMALE GUEST and OLD MALE GUEST are on each side of FRED.

FRED: Alright! Alright! I'm thinking of an animal.

FEMALE GUEST: Is it a savage animal?

FRED: Ferocious!

OLD MALE GUEST: Can it be seen in London, Sir?

FRED: Yes! Yes, indeed!

FEMALE GUEST: In the zoo?

OLD MALE GUEST: In the circus?

FEMALE GUEST: Is it a bear?

FRED: No! Ha! Ha! No! But it growls like one!

FRED moves to chair left.

NARR AS FRED: All, all were laughing, including Scrooge, for what animal could this be?

PRETTY SISTER seated in chair left giggles.

PRETTY SISTER: I know!, I know...

NARR. AS PRETTY SISTER: ...said the pretty sister of Fred's wife.

PRETTY SISTER: ...It's your uncle Scrooge!

Giggle, giggle.

NARR. AS PRETTY SISTER: And all, all had a hearty laugh. All...

NARR. AS SCROOGE: ...except Scrooge.

Bowed cymbal. SCROOGE moves behind chairs.

The whole scene passed off in a breath... *(Scrooge moves down center into city street)* ...and Scrooge and the spirit were once again upon their travels.

Twinkle chime.

NARR. AS SCROOGE: It was a long night and the two saw many remarkable and wonderful things. Scrooge had been so taken by it that he had not noticed until now that the ghost grew older.

SCROOGE: Sweet sir, are spirits lives so short lived?

CHRISTMAS PRESENT steps forward.

CHRISTMAS PRESENT: My life upon this globe is very brief... it ends tonight.

12 clock chimes begin, evenly spaced to the end of the stave.

Hark, the time draws near.

SCROOGE steps back to right side of CHRISTMAS PRESENT. They remain side-by-side throughout scene.

SCROOGE: Forgive me spirit for what I ask, but I see something strange and not belonging to yourself, there, at the bottom of your robe.

CHRISTMAS PRESENT: Oh man! Look here! Look down here!

NARR. AS CHRISTMAS PRESENT: Two small, frail, sullen children held tight to the legs of the ghost.

CHRISTMAS PRESENT: Look at these children, ragged and yellow. Through all the miracles of wonderful creation, how could such shriveled hands cling to these garments. They are man's! This boy is ignorance and this girl is want.

SCROOGE: Have they no refuge? No resource?

CHRISTMAS PRESENT: Are there no prisons? Are there no workhouses?

SCROOGE'S ROOM

NARR. AS SCROOGE: Scrooge looked down in painful guilt and then toward the ghost... But he was alone...

SCROOGE finds himself in his room. Scrooge moves chair (3) to fireplace in Scrooge's room

[DIAGRAM B - fireplace chair order has changed]

...alone... In his dark and lonely room... and he was sorrowfully tired.

END OF ACT I

ACT II

STAVE IV

SCROOGE'S ROOM, FRONT OF FIREPLACE

Sound, 12 clock chimes begin.

1,2,3: lights begin to fade

4,5,6: lights fade out

7,8,9,10: lights fade up

SCROOGE is on the floor in front of the fireplace, asleep.

11,12: SCROOGE awakens with a start.

SCROOGE: Oh No! Spirit? If you are there, I must see you. I must see you. Spirit, if you are there I have learned.

Bowed cymbal.

SCROOGE sees the Ghost. SCROOGE rises, crosses down left, turns and sees the Phantom upstage by fireplace.

NARR. AS SCROOGE: From the shadows, shrouded in a deep black garment, concealing its head and its face and its form, the ghost outstretched its arm.

Bowed cymbal.

SCROOGE: Am I in the presence of the ghost of Christmas yet to come? You are about to show me the shadows of things that have not yet happened—things that might happen? Oh, spirit, though I am well used to ghostly company, I am most frightened by your silent shape. Ghost of the future, I do fear you more than any I have seen but I am prepared to bear your company for the good it will do me. Lead on!

Bowed cymbal.

NARR. AS CHRISTMAS FUTURE: The spirit turned with a sweep of its robe...

SCROOGE follows Phantom into city street: isolated area down left. Chairs do not change.

NARR. AS SCROOGE: ...and Scrooge followed him into the street. They stopped beside a little knot of business men. The great fat man among them spoke out.

FAT MAN: No... I don't know much about it either way. I only know he is dead. He died last night. And what he has done with his money, I haven't heard. Hasn't left it to me! Ha! Ha! Its likely to be a cheap funeral, for upon my life I don't know anybody to go to it. I don't mind going if lunch is provided. Ha! Ha!

NARR. AS SCROOGE: Scrooge knew the big man and wondered...

Bowed cymbal.

SCROOGE crosses up right, places chair (2) down right, isolated area: obscure part of town.

[DIAGRAM I]

...but he and the spirit glided on to an obscure part of town. The whole quarter reeked with crime, with misery and filth. The phantom pointed to a corner...

OLD JOE squats left of chair (3)

[DIAGRAM I]

NARR. AS OLD JOE: ...where a gray-haired rascal of nearly seventy sat... with a familiar woman with a heavy bundle and another who was similarly laden.

OLD JOE: So, If we haven't all met here without meanin' it. Where'd you steal them pickin's luv?

BEGGAR WOMAN is seated next to OLD JOE.

BEGGAR WOMAN: Look here, old Joe! Every person's got a right to take care of themself. He always did!

OLD JOE: Oh! He did! He did! Them's my pickins too. *(To second beggar woman)* And yours?

BEGGAR WOMAN: Well who's the worse for a loss of things like these? Not a dead man. Wicked old screw... Lying there, gasping out his last.

OLD JOE: Ah, Coo!... I missed it!

BEGGAR WOMAN: Well... It's a judgement on him, that's what it is! Look here... sheets, towels, linens... bed curtains, I took em down while he was lying there. I only hope he didn't die of something catchin'.

OLD JOE: Aaagh! He frightened everyone away when he was alive to profit us when he is dead! Ha! Ha!

SCROOGE backs away from chair (3), up right.

SCROOGE: I see! I see, said Scrooge. The case of this unhappy man... might be my own. I need not see any...

Bowed cymbal.

Scrooge backs into chairs (1) & (2): funeral parlor. They represent the casket: isolated area, no chair change.

...merciful heavens, what is this? What is this that is covered up. This ragged sheet bares... Oh, I fear to see! Oh cold, cold, rigid, dreadful death. Spirit, this is a fearful place. In leaving it, I shall not leave its lesson, trust me. Oh, spirit, do not make me lift the shroud! Let us go! Let us go, for I cannot. Spirit, if there is one person in this town who feels some emotion for this man's death, let me see that person.

Bowed cymbal.

NARR. AS CHRISTMAS FUTURE: The phantom spread its robe before them and, in removing it...

Cross down left, poor couple's home: isolated area, no chair change.

NARR. AS YOUNG HUSBAND: ...revealed a room by daylight. A young husband, care worn and depressed, embraced his equally tired and worried young wife. In a serious delight for which he felt shame, he quietly declared.

YOUNG HUSBAND: There is hope! There is hope my sweet Caroline! A miracle has happened! He is dead! He is dead! I found this out when I went to seek a week's delay. I know not who our debt shall be transferred to, but for now our debts and our hearts are lighter. I'm sorry to say but it's a happier home for this man's death.

NARR. AS YOUNG HUSBAND: His arms folded around her and softly, passionately, they shared the moment in joyous relief, and for now we're at peace in each other's warm embrace.

Twinkle chime.

SCROOGE backs out of the scene.

SCROOGE: Is this all... all the tenderness for one mans death?

Bowed cymbal. SCROOGE crosses behind chairs (1) & (2). Scrooge moves chairs stage left creating Cratchit Home.

[DIAGRAM F]

[it is important to note the chair arrangement is now the same as in the previous Cratchit scene but the chair order is different.]

NARR. AS CHRISTMAS FUTURE: The phantom again raised his robe, and in removing it, revealed the dwelling place of Bob Cratchit.

NARR. AS SCROOGE: Scrooge hardly made a sigh and all the Cratchit's were before him...

NARR. AS MRS. CRATCHIT: ...and Mrs. Cratchit, fighting water from her eyes, laid down her handwork.

MRS. CRATCHIT steps forward, puts handwork on chair (3) (chair is facing upstage).

MRS. CRATCHIT: The color hurts my eyes... the color. My poor Tiny Tim. They're better now. It makes them weak by candle light and I would not show weak eyes to your father for the world. OH, where is your father? I have known him to walk very fast. Very fast indeed, with Tiny... *(Mrs. Cratchit sits on sofa, chairs (1) & (2))* ...with Tiny Tim upon his shoulder, but he was so light to carry and his father loved him so.

NARR. AS MRS. CRATCHIT: And all the Cratchit's moved to their mother to console each other.

BOB enters as if coming through back door.

[DIAGRAM F]

NARR. AS BOB: At that moment, Bob came home and saw his sad and solemn family. He too was in need of solace, but with surprising strength, mustered a sweet and generous smile.

BOB: Now, now, we must mind it. Don't be grieved. However and whenever we part from one another, I am sure none of us shall ever forget our poor Tiny Tim, or the first parting there was among us. And we shall not quarrel easily among ourselves. Oh, I'm happy! I'm very happy!

SCROOGE backs out of the house stage right, outside the window.

[DIAGRAM F]

NARR. AS SCROOGE: Scrooge watched as the children kissed their mother and kissed their father and tears swept softly down each and all their sad, loving faces. And he felt empty. He longed to upraise his clerk, indeed to uplift them all.

Bowed cymbal. Graveyard, isolated area on chair (3). SCROOGE rushes into the light around chair (3), down right.

And then the phantom stole the moment into darkness and Scrooge found himself elsewhere yet again in darkness and gloom.

SCROOGE: Specter, I fear our parting is hand... I know it is. Tell me, Specter, who was that man whom we saw lying dead?

SCROOGE looks in the direction the PHANTOM is pointing.

NARR. AS SCROOGE: The spirit pointed to a church yard. Here then was the answer. The wretched man who's name he had to know lay fresh underneath the ground.

Bowed cymbal.

He gradually moves his gaze until it comes to his own feet. The back of chair (3), which is facing upstage is now the headstone of a grave. SCROOGE examines the imaginary gravestone.

SCROOGE: No! No! I will honor Christmas in my heart and keep it all the year. I will live in the past, the present and the future. I will not shut out the lessons they teach. Tell me I may wash away the writing on the stone for I know the name and I wish to make it sweeter.

Twinkle chime. SCROOGE moves chair (3) to right of chair (1) to create bed in scrooge's room (chair order is different).

[DIAGRAM C]

NARR. AS SCROOGE: And with this the phantom shrunk into a familiar bedpost. It was Scrooge's bedpost and dawn was breaking.

SCROOGE examines his bed and discovers he is home.

SCROOGE: What is today? It matters not. It is time to make amends. I will live in the past, present and future, the spirit of all three shall strive with in me.

Church bells.

Oh, Jacob, Jacob Marley, thank you. Heaven and Christmas time be praised; I say it on my knees, I am here! I don't know what to do. I'm as happy as an angel, as light as a feather, as merry as a schoolboy.

NARR. AS SCROOGE: He ran to the window and threw open the pane.

SCROOGE rushes forward to the window and struggles to open it. HE leans outside.

[DIAGRAM C]

SCROOGE: Merry Christmas! Oh! Perhaps I've missed the day, but not in my heart. Merry Christmas!

NARR. AS SCROOGE: He practiced, skillfully, a splendid and most illustrious laugh.

SCROOGE wanders about the room then rushes back to the window.

SCROOGE: Oh! I am quite a baby. I don't know what to do. Whoop! Whoop! Hello! Oh, no fog, no mist, clear, clear, stirring, cold, cold, golden sunlight, heavenly, sweet, fresh air. Glorious! Glorious! *(Scrooge sees Street Boy down right, outside the window)* Boy! Ho boy! What's today boy? What is today my fine young fellow.

STREET BOY steps forward, turns upstage and looks up at SCROOGE.

STREET BOY: Today Sir? You must know, sir! Why, it's Christmas day!

SCROOGE rushes about the room, returning to the window and addressing the boy down right.

NARR. AS SCROOGE: Scrooge was so excited he nearly fell all over himself rushing about, not wanting to miss a moment longer.

SCROOGE: Boy! Do you know the prize turkey hanging in the poulter's shop down the way?

STREET BOY steps forward looks up facing upstage.

STREET BOY: The one that's as big as me?

SCROOGE stares down at the boy.

SCROOGE: Ha! Ha! Remarkable boy! It's a pleasure talking to him. That's the one! Here's half a crown, go and buy it. *(Scrooge watches the boy run from down right to down left and off)* Tell them where to bring it, that I may give them directions where to deliver it. Be back in five minutes and I will give you a shilling. Ha! Ha! Look at him run! Wonderful boy!

SCROOGE (CONT'D): Oh, I have missed so much, but no longer. I shall send it to Bob Cratchit. He musn't know who sends it. Ha! Ha!

SCROOGE crosses stage right as if going to his dressing area.

NARR. AS SCROOGE: The chuckle with which he said this, the chuckle with which he paid for the turkey was only exceeded by the breathless chuckle that made him cry. He dressed himself and...

Door open and close. SCROOGE exits front door down right and wanders into the city street. He crosses into an isolated area down left, no chair change.

...went down into the street and by chance, greeted the gentlemen who had previously required charity from him.

SCROOGE addresses the two imaginary gentlemen.

SCROOGE: Forgive me kind sirs! I know you fear my pleasantness but I beg your forgiveness and ask you to be at ease for I am of a new spirit. And please except from me, for charity, a donation in the amount of... *(Whispering into one of the gentlemen's ear)* ...Yes! Yes! A Great many back payments are required... and needed. Merry Christmas! Will you come and see me... will you?

SCROOGE then vigorously shakes each of their hands.

NARR. AS SCROOGE: And with happy business done, he bid them the best of the season and then he went to church.

Church bells ring.

SCROOGE turns around. he is in the same place as before, for church bells ring. When the bells stop, Scrooge turns forward. He crosses to stage right as if wandering through the city.

And following the service and after many glad encounters, he wandered through the streets watching the people rushing to and fro. He patted little children on their heads. He found everything could bring him pleasure.

CRATCHIT HOME

SCROOGE moves chair (3) beside the down right front door. The arrangement is Cratchit's house.

[DIAGRAM F - different chair order]

NARR. AS SCROOGE: Then... then, he decided to stop by Bob Cratchit's house and through the window enjoyed the turkey as much or more than Bob and his family and all from this unobserved distance. Then... then, he stopped at his nephews, smiling and humble.

SCROOGE moves chairs (1) & (2) to beside door in Fred's house, chair (3) remains downstage right.

[DIAGRAM H]

SCROOGE: Good afternoon. It is I, your uncle Scrooge. I have come to dinner. Will you let me in Fred?

NARR. AS SCROOGE: Let him in! Let him in! *(Scrooge is pulled center stage)* It was a miracle Fred didn't shake his arm off. And all the guests welcomed him, and he sang and danced and played guessing games with all the rest... and complimented the hostess on a more than delightful dinner. Never did anyone enjoy the day as much as Scrooge. And when evening fell he bid them all farewell... and a Merry Christmas... *(Scrooge exits Fred's house through front door)* ...and went home to bed and slept like a new infant to the world.

SCROOGE enters counting house into his office through front door.

[DIAGRAM A]

Upon the following morning...

Door open and close. SCROOGE moves chair (2) to BOB's work place (original chair 3).

[DIAGRAM A]

...Scrooge arrived early to his office... and as luck would have it, found Bob Cratchit was behind his time ...

SCROOGE moves chair (3) to SCROOGE's work place, facing upstage (original chair 2)

[DIAGRAM A]

...and for once Scrooge was happy about it. Just as Scrooge had settled...

BOB rushes in counting house door.

NARR. AS BOB: ...Bob came rushing in... *(Door open and close)* And, seeing Scrooge, he quietly and most respectfully moved to speak.

BOB: I am sorry, sir! Very sorry!

SCROOGE steps left of BOB.

SCROOGE: Yes! I should think you are! Come this way, sir! I am not going to stand for this a moment longer. Therefore, Bob Cratchit—

NARR. AS SCROOGE: —Scrooge had to pinch himself to keep from laughing—

SCROOGE: —I am about to... raise your salary! Ha! Ha! Ha!

BOB steps center stage, frozen.

NARR. AS BOB: Bob had a thought to call for people in the courtyard, and for a straight waistcoat.

SCROOGE steps left, embarrassed.

SCROOGE: I have been a fool, Bob! I will raise your salary and endeavor to assist your struggling family.

SCROOGE (CONT'D): We shall talk about it this afternoon over a Christmas bowl. In the meantime, make us a couple of warm fires and buy another coal scuttle before you dot another "i."

BOB steps center, frozen.

NARR. AS BOB: Bob was stunned and could not move. *(Bob falls off balance)* Scrooge had to nudge him to get him started, to which both men began a low laugh which grew to a truthful, uproarious, generous embrace. And both men were grateful...

BOB tentatively shakes SCROOGE's hand. SCROOGE vigorously shakes BOB's hand.

NARR. AS SCROOGE: ...to the other.

Twinkle chime.

NARRATOR (ACTOR AS SELF) faces the audience.

NARRATOR: Scrooge was better than his word! And Tiny Tim did not die! Scrooge became as good as any man in any good old city in the good old world. He knew how to celebrate Christmas if any man alive possessed the knowledge.

SCROOGE crosses back to his desk.

NARR. AS SCROOGE: His heart laughed, and that was enough for him and he always remembered what Tiny Tim had said...

SCROOGE turns in his chair, leaning toward the audience.

SCROOGE: God bless us, everyone!

SCROOGE faces upstage, furiously and joyfully working. He sings:

(Singing)

GOD REST YE MERRY GENTLEMEN
LET NOTHING YOU DISMAY
REMEMBER CHRIST OUR SAVIOR
WAS BORN ON CHRISTMAS DAY
TO SAVE US ALL FROM SATAN'S POWER
WHEN WE HAD GONE ASTRAY
OH, TIDINGS OF COMFORT AND JOY
COMFORT AND JOY
OH, TIDINGS OF COMFORT AND...

SCROOGE extends his arm up into the air, mirroring TINY TIM from earlier at the dining table.

...JOY!

Twinkle chime. Lights fade to black.

END

ABOUT STAGE RIGHTS

Based in Los Angeles and founded in 2000, Stage Rights is one of the foremost independent theatrical publishers in the United States, providing stage performance rights for a wide range of plays and musicals to theater companies, schools, and other producing organizations across the country and internationally. As a licensing agent, Stage Rights is committed to providing each producer the tools they need for financial and artistic success. Stage Rights is dedicated to the future of live theatre, offering special programs that champion new theatrical works.

To view all of our current plays and musicals, visit:

www.stagerights.com

Printed in Great Britain
by Amazon

47927669R00025